Ubiquitous Honey Bee

Melissa Folen

BookLeaf Publishing

India | USA | UK

DEDICATION

To my beautiful daughter Sissy Bella, you're more than I could have dreamed of.

To my fierce, brave son Sebastian, your knowledge and spirit inspires me to be a better a human.

To my soft hearted XY, you completed in me what I didn't know was missing.

You three are my greatest accomplishment. What I see in you, makes me whole.

ACKNOWLEDGEMENT

Philippians 4:8-14

8Finally, brethren, whatsoever things are true, whatsoever things are honest, whatsoever things are just, whatsoever things are pure, whatsoever things are lovely, whatsoever things are of good report; if there be any virtue, and if there be any praise, think on these things. 9Those things, which ye have both learned, and received, and heard, and seen in me, do: and the God of peace shall be with you. 10But I rejoiced in the Lord greatly, that now at the last your care of me hath flourished again; wherein ye were also careful, but ye lacked opportunity. 11Not that I speak in respect of want: for I have learned, in whatsoever state I am, therewith to be content. 12I know both how to be abased, and I know how to abound: every where and in all things I am instructed both to be full and to be hungry, both to abound and to suffer need. 13I can do all things through Christ which strengtheneth me. 14Notwithstanding ye have well done, that ye did communicate with my affliction.

PREFACE

A collection of thoughts, moments and
emotions.

Yadah, My Earth Angel

I met a stranger who changed my life,
she was a prayer answered to burden and strife.

I know that God sent her, so I wouldn't face
alone,
the inward struggle to find a place called home.

Chaos ensued me, I was a weary soul,
But a seed was planted, allowing me to grow.

I pondered the question, is there a heart like
mine,
she was delivered, predestined, divine.

I peeled back layers I held onto so long,
realizing I needed a presence that was just as
strong.

I met my earth angel as it was planned,
finally understanding I can trust this hand.

God knew my heart, my defeat, my despair,
and sent me a human capable of care.

To see my journey is to understand grace,

given to me by God, with an earth angel I can't replace.

Time

Is life a reality or just a bad dream,
Do you really exist and are things what they
seem?
What would you do if all time stopped,
And on your shoulders the burden of the world
was dropped.

How would you breathe if all the air was gone,
Would you find a way to survive, would you
stand alone?
Do distant thoughts ever enter your mind,
Do you think of the one you love, or the one you
left behind?

Do you feel caged up inside of yourself,
Knowing you're forever going to be by yourself?
Do you look in the mirror and wonder who it is
you see,
Is it the person you are or the person you wanted
to be?

Does your soul ever drift in to another place,
Is it better there or the same problems you
already faced?
Do you ever want to escape, is there a way,

Time does not stop for feelings; it drags on
every day.

Can you accomplish the desires of your heart,
Or are you one of the weaker ones that will get
torn apart?
And when you think everything is alright and
you're going to succeed,
You realize what you have is not what you need.

Life

It's sad life tragically ends,
It's over as soon as it begins.

It's hard knowing you were born to die,
You learn to love and then say goodbye.

Everyone is searching for their soul mate,
Yet hearts are broken, love is a debate.

Like a cigarette burning down to its last draw,
Decisions you make will rise and fall.

Laughter ends, the fun is gone,
Now you're searching for the place you belong.

You call in to the night, raging against your
being,
Life is what you make of it, but your eyes are
not seeing.

Tick tock tick tock time goes on,
You feel your desires fading, your reality is
gone.

Journey

To forgive, one must be strong,
You have to face where you don't belong.

The snare of internal battles, depth to the deep,
I am my father's child, his promises he does
keep.

I speak of a grace that came like the softest hug,
Looking at my past, on my heart he did tug.

Offering to me forgiveness, broken now whole,
The roads we traveled no one knows.

I was a wretched thing, dirty and despaired,
He met me in my mess, showed me he cared.

Although audibly, I have never heard his voiced,
He imprinted on me, his way, I made my choice.

This world has forsaken me time and again,
He gave me the opportunity to begin.

This is not battle in the physical sense,
It is spiritual warfare that is intense.

One must be dexterous, and tread with care,
We must make a difference, our testimony share.

Keeper; Song (Him/Her)

Him:

There's a lot of fish in the sea,
But there was only one keeper for me.
She had a smile that said lifetime,
And her eyes could actually hold mine.

I kept coming around until she let down her
guard,
I never worked for a girl so hard.
But just like the hands of time,
I let her slip right through mine.

Stopped paying attention to the little things,
That use to make her heart sing.
She was an extraordinary girl,
Living in an ordinary world.

She held it down like the family stone,
Willing to walk the roads alone.
Told her she could fly, then I clipped her wings,
She smiled and said this to me.

Her:

I gave you a key to a locked door,
One I said I wouldn't give away anymore.
Told you there was a lot of trouble inside,
Let downs that I tried hide.

A lot of people thought that they were game,
But it ended just the same.
I won't settle for less than I deserve,
I don't grade on a teacher's curve.

You have to be as strong as me,
See through the eyes that I see.
You got to battle right beside me,
I don't need you to save me.

I am not a damsel in distress,
If you look closely, you'll see an "S" on my
chest.
If you can't step up, then step out,
Cause a shadow of a man isn't what I'm about.

Him:

I look back and realize,
How I was the one in disguise.
She laid it down for me and kept it real,
She gave my heart an invitation to finally feel.

I gave her two seconds of the best of me,
Just a glimpse so she could really see,
The type of man I could really be,
Then she met the other side of me.

She threw her hands up one day,
Told me the things that I needed to do to make
her stay.
I listened with deaf ears as she walked away,
I still regret that to this day.

Inside my head I was screaming,
Battling all the pent-up demons.
I could have sworn I heard her angels sing,
As she turned around and spread her wings.

I think about her every day,
Wish I would made the changes to make her
stay.
She changed the locks on that closed door, and
threw my key on the floor,
Said I am not welcome there anymore.

That girl taught me how to be free,
To see the depths inside of me.
She's gone and here I stand,
Went from a player to a man.

If I could turn back the hands of time,

That girl would still be mine.

Trust

When I look at you, I see me,
I see the love you cast away, and the fears you
see.

In your life when you have tried to trust,
The people you thought you knew, went from
gold to dust.

I know what it feels like when all hope is gone,
I have walked down many roads and stood
alone.

In a suit, as if you were a clown,
You play that role for everyone around.

I see the distance in your eyes when you look
away,
You keep your emotions held in, your thoughts
at bay.

Putting the world at a distance, it's easy to
survive,
If you let anyone get to close, they could bury
you alive.

You can be a friend, that's not an act,
But the memories of the past still attack.

We've both traveled a road that has not been
kind,
But in this process we've cleared the mind.

It was the journey to who we are,
And that dear one is more than our scars.

Darkest Dreams

I come to you in your darkest dreams,
Life is eternal or so it seems.

I stay to myself trying to avoid trust,
Yet people turn to me, my opinion is a must.

I give advice, I never take,
I open up to no one, is this my mistake?

How can I save others when I walk alone,
I have forsaken myself, my passions are gone.

I walk in the shadow, I avoid the pain,
For all the love I have pushed away, I have
nothing to gain.

Lightning strikes and it entices me,
Thunder collides my body, it sets my soul free.

At night I wonder if there is a reason I am still
here,
Is my life just beginning or are death clouds
near?

Should I let others in to my life,

Should I open someone else up to my world of
strife?

Should I just go on,
and forever roam alone.

And then when all the darkness ends,
I open my eyes, a new day begins.

Yesterday

When I stop and think about yesterday, the tears slowly shield my eyes,
I remember seeing your face and your oh so sweet goodbyes.

The times we once had slowly drifted away,
Now I am living in the past because I can't live without you today.

Friends all around saying you're no good,
I never listened to them it was by your side I stood.

Now I think about all the advice they gave,
For all the tears I cried, it was my heart I could not save.

Now your nowhere, you're blowing in the wind,
Everyone was right, all we had never began.

For your one night of loneliness, I have a life time to feel,
You broke my heart in two, what was fake I thought was real.

Needless to say I still think about you at night,
I still feel you in my heart, I still see you in my
sight.

Our love is over, it will never be the same,
In your mind it was all an easy-going game.

The One

Off in the distance, things seem bleak,
But still I push on, standing in my meek.

Loudness left me as life humbled,
I fought and walked, even though I stumbled.

I keep the faith that things will be,
As the one who protects promised me.

Not about materials, those do not feed the soul,
The things that bring peace, softness from the
one I know.

The one who can, always and ever shining,
I felt the loves blanket, even when the dark is
climbing.

I battled the way only a true heart can do,
I called out your name and worshiped you.

I keep the oil in the lamp for the day you come,
Most cherished amongst men, you are the one.

Death could not keep you, your value was more,
You are the key to every locked door.

As Remembered

A kiss gently placed,
On a face that is filled with grace.

A smile to remember, eyes of blue,
The angel in my arms is a memory of you.

You gave me hope, you gave me laughter,
Then took away my ever after.

For all the pain that we went through,
I was still left with the best part of you.

You sent an angel, with your eyes,
To lay close to me, I tend to his cries.

One day I'll teach him to be a man,
And about his father try to make him
understand.

There will be questions, tears will be shed,
But I'll be the one there to tuck him in to bed.

All the love he will have, will be no surprise,
But he will also learn to see life through a
woman's eyes.

I'll teach him to care and always be honest,
That's what you lacked, for this he must
promise.

So even though you left, you're with me every
day,
He's the one love you can't take away.

Cherish

Cherish the memories, remember the times,
When friends were real and love was kind.

Forget the tears, forget the pain,
Remember the sunshine goes on after the rain.

Strength comes through when you are weak,
It's an unheard voice that learns to speak.

Slowly awakening, find your poise,
Push back against it, quiet the noise.

You'll never know what you can do,
Until the world around you depends on you.

Crack your backbone, prepare for the fight,
That may go long in to a treacherous night.

As you take these steps, arm yourself well,
Be prepared for the backlash of hell.

A warrior's stance, a battle-ready heart,
The curve of her smile, she was born for this
part.

Remember eye of the tiger, find your fight,
The pain can be there, but master it for spite.

Find the passion from deep inside,
And let that be the laws to which you abide.

Know that it's okay when you fall,
As long as you rise back up and stand tall.

Don't be afraid if you try and fail,
Being timid is a weakness that never prevails.

Voice your opinion, state your claim,
Be heard in the world, show your flame.

If you burn out, you can light again,
With each new day, it's a new chance to begin.

This world can make you angry, people can
make you sad,
But don't let it destroy you, let it make you mad.

When you realize it's just a stronghold that you
can control,
Then you will have it in you to let go.

Believe in who you are, keep your dreams alive,
And always follow your heart, that's how you
will survive.

Comfort

On the wings of a bird is how you send your prayer,
You know God is listening, he's always there.

When times get bad and you feel like you can't go on,
Tune your spirit in to his song.

When your heart aches, he's there to comfort the pain,
He's the sunshine when all you see is rain.

He is the strength that speaks just a little bit more,
You can do this, walk through the door.

Don't give up, don't give in,
Rest softly in the protection of him.

I know it's not perfect, it was never meant to be,
But a promise was made for those who believe.

Beautiful minds can't wrap themselves around worldly ways,
It sets one up for demise and decay.

Strive to show kindness, be diligent and aware,
Set yourself apart from the world that does not
care.

Only then can you truly embrace,
The love you've been given, the abundance of
grace.

Lessons

What is this taste, I've seen it before,
It is the remembrance of a long-lost door.

I walk up to it, remembering the lesson of its
pain,
Grasping at multiple realities, but they all ended
the same.

It doesn't feel like it was that long ago,
That hell broke loose and I got lost in the tow.

I carry those scars across my heart,
Things are better now but I won't ever forget that
part.

The art of healing is acknowledging the hurt,
Recognizing without you letting it go, you bury
yourself in the dirt.

I know what is required of me, and what I must
do,
To heal the line, make the tribe brand new.

I have to confront every darkness with the power
of light,

Only one I know can shine this bright.

He is where true forgiveness lies,
I accepted him and said my goodbyes.

Goodbye to never being enough,
I knew this journey would make me tough.

Broken

Broken, a word that is vacant and cold,
A word that my reality must hold.

No time for laughter, no time for tears,
A world set aside consumed by unforeseen fears.

A ray of light, I blow it out,
Can't let someone in who will bring more doubt.

Speaking the truth such an odd thing,
Not use to hearing words of kindness sing.

Baffled and bruised from all that life has
bestowed,
Looking a smile in the face but choosing the
cold.

Stripping myself bare closing the door,
I have the heart that can take no more.

No more bitterness, no more screams in the
night,
No more open eyes that have lost their sight.

Protecting myself from anymore blows,

Wrapping myself in reality my blood begins to
flow.

I will push forward like nothing is wrong,
Standing indefinitely in the shadows where no
one belongs.

Strong enough to know that I will lose the fight,
Pushing laughter away, saying no to the light.

I could have been happy, I could have been so
much more,
If I had taken up for myself and closed the right
door.

Life I'll taste it just a bit,
But I will not be the one who will ever submit.

Child Of

I held my head low as I walked in the place,
Not belonging here long ago fell from grace

I was welcomed by stranger's eyes,
The warmth that I felt held no disguise

I began thinking maybe I could be,
A child of God, one who has been set free

From all the burdens of life's past mistakes,
Hand it all over whatever it takes

I went to places I did not want to go,
I ask for forgiveness from a long dark road

I saw the light it captured me,
From a long hard road traveled in solitary.

It may look like I stand alone,
But I am with God it where I belong

To many days past before I could see,
I needed God to find joy inside of me

With my sins cast aside I became whole,

Loving the giant inside of me that I did not
know

I held my head high as I walked out of the place,
I began my new life living in grace

The Fall

I fell down, to a place I did not know I could go,
But the ground was soft when it caught me from
below.

I realized this was the place I needed to be,
I realized by falling this fall I was where I could
truly see.

I needed to taste the bitter feeling of a life gone
wrong,
To empower me to once again become strong.

I did not fight the tears, I shed them with pride,
They tore down the walls from which behind I
was trying to hide.

This place is familiar, yes, I know the taste,
All of the things coming down in a reality I had
not faced.

I did not think it would be so easy to let go,
But inside a woman, is a strength no man knows.

The strength to prevail on even the worst days,

When you feel battered and beaten, somehow
you find a way.

Even in destruction, there is a chance to rebuild,
a demolished heart can be healed.

This is a lesson I had to learn,
even though I feel the consequence of a slow
burn.

In realizing that no one's perfect, no one at all,
I see the significance of my fall.

Mom

I shed a tear as I remember the woman that
taught me how to smile,
The one that I thought would be by my side, as I
walked every mile.

The one who was as free as the wind,
The one that gave her all, right up until the end.

I didn't understand her as well then as I do today,
Now I face the obstacles she dealt with every
day.

I remember what it felt like to receive a
meaningful hug,
One that was kind, warm, and embraced with
undying love.

I remember the way she use to look at us, now I
understand,
I look at my babies the same way, the way only
a mom can.

I remember happiness, she always took my side,
When I needed comfort, it was in her I could
confide.

She was the shelter that protected me from the
all that was bad,
I didn't get to say goodbye, I opened my eyes,
and memories were all I had.

I didn't get to say I am sorry for making her cry
the day she drove away,
I would take it back, but now I live with it every
day.

I would choose you mom, I would walk through
the flames,
If just for one more second, I could hear you call
my name.

You are the spirit I carry inside me, The
forgiveness I have in my heart,
In every aspect of my life you still take part.

It's the memory of you that makes my smile
genuine and my soul sweet,
You raised me the way I will raise my kids, in
that you'll never be beat.

You had the heart of a champion and kindness
that I have not seen since you died,
When the world hit you the hardest, you still
tried.

You will never know what you meant to me, or
the tears I cry at night,
How I want to scream because I thought your
timing wasn't right.

How can I say thank you for life, for every part
of me,
When I look in the mirror, it's your eyes see.

Thank you for the boys, they are your greatest
gift,
Without them I would not have made it through
such an awful rift.

Seeing you in them kept a smile on my face,
That's a part of you no one can replace.

You are my mom, you always will be,
You'll always be the part of me that is free.

Photograph In Our Mind

Let's make a memory, a photograph in our mind,
When we smiled at each other and our words
were kind.

Let's blush together at the crazy things we did,
And forget all the awful words said.

Let's leave the past behind us, and just walk
away,
If we see each other on the street, no hi, hello's
or hey.

Let's rewind the last little bit, and keep our
secret place,
The one where we can go to, that no-one else
can replace.

Let's not dwell, because it wasn't what we
thought it would be,
Let's leave it as an innocent memory.

Let's not pretend we know who the other is in
any way,
Let's just keep the silence, as we walk away.

Let's remember the smiles, and the laughter,
But let's realize there will be no happily
ever-after.

I say let's because I needed it that way,
I wasn't so naive that I thought you'd stay.

The perfection is busted, the pedestal is no more,
Words whispered in my ear pushed me out the
door.

I would not give up on something that I thought
could be,
But I won't be anyone's doormat, that's just not
me.

I won't look in your eyes, I won't see your heart,
I won't punish myself for not being able to take
part.

I won't be the smile on your face,
But I will be the girl you keep in a secret place.

The one who believed in you, more than words
can say,
the one who would have stood by your side
every day.

The one who would fight the darkness that
plagued you at night,
The one who would have held you close to take
away the fright.

The one who would take the anger, and put a
smile back on your face,
The one who would've filled the void of a dark,
empty place.

But I am not the girl for you, you don't see me,
And I can't take the silence, so just set me free.

Us

Can you hear me, I am the voice telling you to
stay strong,
Can you see me, I am the vision showing you
where you belong.

Can you feel me, I am the gentle breeze across
your skin,
Can you understand me, I am where you begin.

Can you stand me, in the depths of your soul,
Can you walk me through the places you said no
one would ever go.

Can you remember the laughter after the joke is
long gone,
Can you take a chance that I might turn out
wrong.

Can visualize me standing in the shadow of the
darkness of your heart,
Can it be me that helps get you over this part.

Can you take baby steps back into life,
Can you hold on to me and let go of the strife.

Can you find a balance of darkness and light,
Can you realize they are the same, they make
each other right.

Can you pretend it was never the way it was,
Can you honestly say that there was never an
"us".

Knock, Knock

Knock, knock can I come in,
I could be the beginning or the end.

Am I chance your willing to take,
or will I pay for past mistakes?

Did it occur to you that you could lose control,
It wouldn't phase me, no one else would know.

Maybe I don't like perfect, maybe I like
imperfection,
That is why I am so guarded in my own
selection.

I like different, not the common thing,
Fire in my belly, the stuff that love could bring.

Hmmm..run away, that's what you'll do,
For some reason I bring out the coward in you.

Push as hard as you can, you have to nothing
gain,
Good luck in the ignorance of thinking your
avoiding pain.

Stop, I'm done,
The battle is over, but the war has just begun.

Hmmm.....Could this be,
That I am the woman who is finally setting
herself free.

Decide

I cannot walk this mile for you, But I will be
your friend,
It will be your choice if this is the end.

You have to decide if how it is, is the way you
always want it to be,
It's your choice, if you choose, you can always
be free.

You can drink the pain away just like you always
do,
Or you can see that there is a mountain of worth
inside you.

Being bent is different from being broken, you
can rebuild,
And even though you have a demolished heart, it
can be healed.

You can learn to trust again, not everyone will
do you wrong,
And if you open yourself up, you might find out
where you belong.

I am no one, I have nothing to gain,

I just want you to know, the sunshine will outlast
rain.

It won't be like this forever, what you going
through,
But your gonna have to cowboy up, and find the
fight in you.

I don't want to see you unhappy, I hope you find
true love,
I pray that God rains down blessings for you
from up above.

I hope that your heart is always filled with
laughter, and a smile is always on your face,
You deserve every chance in life, and you need
to remember everyone falls from grace.

No one's perfect, everyone makes mistakes, in
life that's a given,
But you have to realize, for those mistakes you
are forgiven.

You can let it eat you up, or you realize that you
deserve more,
All it takes is turning around and opening a
different door.

I am not saying this for me, I don't know you
anymore,
And it's alright that you chose to shut that door.

You will always be a good memory, not tainted
in any way,
I say good-luck to you, be happy, but I let you
go today.